The Power
of the Seed

Inkwell Heritage
Publishing
18896 Greenwell Springs Road
Greenwell Springs, LA 70739

The Power
of the Seed

Understanding How God's Kingdom Works

by

Andrea "Andy" McDougal

Published by:

Inkwell Heritage Publishing
18896 Greenwell Springs Road
Greenwell Springs, LA 70739

ISBN 989-8-9987460-4-8

Printed on demand in the US, the UK and Australia
For Worldwide Distribution

While the earth remains, seedtime and harvest, cold and heat, summer and winter, and day and night shall not cease.

— Genesis 8:22

Be careful what you are hearing. The measure of thought and study you give to the truth you hear will be the measure of virtue and knowledge that comes back to you.
— Mark 4:24

Other Books
by Andy McDougal

Contents

About the Cover

I have selected the sunflower as the image to grace the cover of this book because that flower produces more seeds per plant than any other, up to two thousand.

Mark 4:1-12

Again Jesus began to teach beside the lake. And a very great crowd gathered about Him, so that He got into a ship in order to sit in it on the sea, and the whole crowd was at the lakeside on the shore. And He taught them many things in parables (illustrations or comparisons put beside truths to explain them), and in His teaching He said to them:

Give attention to this! Behold, a sower went out to sow. And as he was sowing, some seed fell along the path, and the birds came and ate it up. Other seed [of the same kind] fell on ground full of rocks, where it had not much soil; and at once it sprang up, because it had no depth of soil; and when the sun came up, it was scorched, and because it had not taken root, it withered away. Other seed [of the same kind] fell among thorn plants, and the thistles grew and pressed together and utterly choked and suffocated it, and it yielded no grain.

And other seed [of the same kind] fell into good (well-adapted) soil and brought forth grain, growing up and increasing, and yielded up to thirty times as much, and sixty times as much, and even a hundred times as much as had been sown. And He said, He who has ears to hear, let him be hearing [and let him consider, and comprehend].

And as soon as He was alone, those who were around Him, with the Twelve [apostles], began to ask Him about the parables. And He said to them, To you has been entrusted the mystery of the kingdom of God [that is, the secret counsels of God which are hidden from the ungodly]; but for those outside [of our circle] everything becomes a parable, in order that they may [indeed] look and look but not see and perceive, and may hear and hear but not grasp and comprehend, lest haply they should turn again, and it [their willful rejection of the truth] should be forgiven them.

UNDERSTAND THE POTENTIAL OF THE SEED AND YOU CAN BENEFIT FROM ITS POWER. THAT IS THE MESSAGE OF THIS BOOK!

Introduction

There is incredible power in a small seed. Farmers know it well and depend on that power for their livelihood. Each year, they faithfully prepare the ground available to them and then sow into it seeds that often look little or nothing like the fruit that will eventually appear as a result of their planting. Farmers do this by faith because they know the creative power that God has invested in each tiny seed. To the layman, each harvest seems like a miracle.

There are other kinds of seeds that God sows into us, and, given the proper care and nourishment, those seeds will also produce a miraculous harvest. Understand the potential of the seed and you can benefit from its power. That is the message of this book. If you can understand how seeds work and how that relates to God's Kingdom, you can reap a harvest of all that you need to prosper in this life and the life to come—spiritually, financially, and emotionally. Get excited and begin to anticipate what God desires to do for you.

Before you begin, however, I want to invite you to do some preparation for the message you are about to read. I often say, when I am about to minister anywhere in person, that those of us who have gathered in that particular place have done so "to do Kingdom business." I am convinced that this is no less true when the message is being relayed in book form. Reading this book is an important moment in your life. You are about to cross a threshold and enter into something new and wonderful, and you need to get ready for that.

The seed we want to explore in the pages of this book is not just what God sows into you. In a very real sense, *you* are a seed, and it is important that you are sown into good soil. The Scriptures teach us:

> *I assure you, most solemnly I tell you, Unless a grain of wheat falls into the earth and dies, it remains [just one grain; it never becomes more but lives] by itself alone. But if it dies, it produces many others and yields a rich harvest.*
>
> John 12:24

What happens with a seed when it is planted *is* a miracle, and that same miracle is waiting for you

THE SEED WE WANT
TO EXPLORE IN THE
PAGES OF THIS BOOK IS
NOT JUST WHAT GOD
SOWS INTO YOU. IN A
VERY REAL SENSE, YOU
ARE A SEED, AND IT IS
IMPORTANT THAT YOU
ARE SOWN INTO GOOD
SOIL.

when you get your seed [yourself] firmly planted in good soil. Something is about to happen on the inside of you that will bear a tremendous amount of fruit and will help catapult you into a greater realm of personal anointing and ministry.

Right now, allow God to break up any fallow ground in your heart. If you are burdened down with problems or concerns of any type, let God free you of them now so that you can soar in His Spirit as He desires. What is hindering you might be discouragement, disappointment, hurt or anger. Whatever it is, let God deal with it now. Give it to Him, for you don't want anything to hinder you from becoming part of His great army in the earth today.

Your voice will soon be heard in the earth. Your destiny is before you right now. If the enemy has caused things to be withheld from you, now is the time that God will cause a loosening of those things, so that you can become all that you have been called to be in this present life.

If you can think of something in your life that would hinder you from receiving all that God wants to do for you, repent of it right now, and ask Him to forgive you. Pray this prayer with me now in preparation for receiving His blessing:

Introduction

Father, in the name of Jesus, I repent before You for allowing the little foxes to come in and spoil my vines. I repent of every sin, of anything and everything that I have done which has caused a hindrance between You and me. I thank You for the blood of the Lamb, and I ask that Your precious blood would cover my heart this day. Let that powerful blood be applied and do the work that only it can.

Father, I choose to forgive any person I have held something against. [Pray this with boldness and sincerity.] *I forgive any person who has offended me or hurt me in any way. And I thank You, Father, that You are setting me free right now from unforgiveness. Thank You that the blood of the Lamb has now covered me, and I am cleansed and made whole. I now have total victory.*

Amen!

Now, please take a few minutes and thank the Lord in your own words for what He is doing in you before moving on with the rest of the book.

Andrea "Andy" McDougal
Baton Rouge, Louisiana

PART I

*Understanding
Jesus' Teachings*

CHAPTER 1

Initiated into the Mysteries

Again Jesus began to teach beside the lake. And a very great crowd gathered about Him, so that He got into a ship in order to sit in it on the sea, and the whole crowd was at the lakeside on the shore. And He taught them many things in parables (illustrations or comparisons put beside truths to explain them).   Mark 4:1-2

Jesus' teaching that is given in Mark 4 is also recorded in Matthew 13. There the disciples wanted to know why Jesus spoke in parables, making it difficult for those outside of the Kingdom to understand. Matthew 13:11 recorded Jesus' reply:

And He replied to them, To you it has been given to know the secrets and mysteries of the kingdom of heaven, but to them it has not been given. For whoever has [spiritual knowledge], to him will

23

*more be given and he will be furnished richly so
that he will have abundance; but from him who
has not, even what he has will be taken away.
This is the reason that I speak to them in parables:
because having the power of seeing, they do not
see; and having the power of hearing, they do not
hear, nor do they grasp and understand.*

Matthew 13:11

Jesus mentioned here *"the secrets and mysteries"* of His Kingdom. These secrets and mysteries, or *mustirios* in Greek, were the sacred secrets. This meant that they were hidden and held in reserve until the appropriate time when God would unveil them. These mysteries were then to be made known to those who had teachable spirits.

The Word is very specific here. It says that these sacred secrets have been *given* or granted to those of us who love the Lord. If you have a teachable heart, then the mysteries of the Kingdom, the sacred secrets, belong to you.

Jesus went on to explain why there were mysteries, sacred secrets, things held in reserve, kept from common knowledge. In verse 12, He said:

*For whoever has [spiritual knowledge], to him
will more be given and he will be furnished richly
so that he will have abundance; but from him who
has not, even what he has will be taken away.*

THE WORD IS VERY SPECIFIC HERE. IT SAYS THAT THESE SACRED SECRETS HAVE BEEN *GIVEN* OR GRANTED TO THOSE OF US WHO LOVE THE LORD!

Of those who could not receive His teaching, Jesus said:

Having the power of seeing, they do not see; and having the power of hearing, they do not hear, nor do they grasp and understand. Matthew 13:13

The reason for this was that they were not part of God's Kingdom. Because their hearts were not teachable, they could not yet comprehend these truths. Therefore, these mysteries would be withheld from them until they entered into and became part of the Kingdom.

What exactly are the mysteries or *mustirios* of God? This word *mustirio* means "to be initiated into." Every time you read the Word of God and revelation is opened up to you, without you even being aware of it, you are being initiated into the Word of God and into His Kingdom mysteries.

That word *initiated* is very powerful. Through the *mustirios* of God, we are initiated into the mysteries of God because we have teachable hearts and it, therefore, has been granted to us to have access to secret Kingdom knowledge.

The word *initiation* is "the act of admitting someone into a secret." That's what happens when we start understanding God's mysteries.

That word *initiate* also means "to begin at a new starting point." Therefore, when you are initiated into a new revelation of God's Word, that new revelation brings a new beginning to your life. You are understanding or comprehending something you didn't understand or comprehend before, and the result is that a new beginning has been initiated in your life through that revelation.

Another meaning for *mustirios*, the sacred secrets, is "something previously hidden but now revealed, doctrine that in the past has not been fully made known." I love Paul's references to the mystery of grace:

> *For this reason because I preached that you are thus built up together], I, Paul, [am] the prisoner of Jesus the Christ for the sake and on behalf of you Gentiles — assuming that you have heard of the stewardship of God's grace (His unmerited favor) that was entrusted to me [to dispense to you] for your benefit, and] that the mystery (secret) was made known to me and I was allowed to comprehend it by direct revelation, as I already briefly wrote you.* Ephesians 3:1-3

This mystery of God's grace had been withheld until Paul came on the scene. For generations, century after century, God had kept this secret … until the moment He revealed it to Paul, a man with a teachable heart.

AS YOU ARE INITIATED INTO THE MYSTERIES OF GOD, SOMETHING IS INITIATED OR SET IN MOTION IN YOUR LIFE!

Initiated into the Mysteries

How amazing is that? The grace of God had remained a mystery for thousands of years until Paul came on the scene and God revealed it to him and then, through him, to all mankind.

As you are initiated into the mysteries of God, something is initiated or set in motion in your life. All of us need for God to set things in motion, and when we are initiated into new revelations from God's Word, that initiation of movement and action begins. God sets something in motion in our lives and begins to propel us forward.

CHAPTER 2

"Be Careful What You Are Hearing!"

And He said to them, Be careful what you are hearing. The measure [of thought and study] you give [to the truth you hear] will be the measure [of virtue and knowledge] that comes back to you—and more [besides] will be given to you who hear.   Mark 4:24

Before we continue with the earlier part of Mark 4, I want us to examine this verse 24, for it is the key to our understanding of the entire passage. Look at it again:

Be careful what you are hearing. The measure [of thought and study] you give [to the truth you

31

hear] will be the measure [of virtue and knowl-
edge] that comes back to you.

In this scripture, the Lord has just given us some powerful keys. When these words first caught my attention, I pondered them day and night for weeks. Even when I was upon my bed, I could not get them out of my spirit.

This is so important. We cannot be too careful about what we hear. Also, the way we react to the Word of God and the way we yield to it (or not) is important. The way we study it (or not) and meditate on it (or not) is also important. This will all determine what is measured back to us as a result.

The next verse shows us just how important this truth is:

For to him who has will more be given; and from
him who has nothing, even what he has will be
taken away [by force].   Mark 4:25

Those who are careful about what they hear and what they study and mediate on will receive even more. Those who are careless in this regard will have less. Even what they now have will be

EVEN WHEN I WAS UPON MY BED, I COULD NOT GET THESE WORDS OUT OF MY SPIRIT!

taken from them. This is monumental in our lives, as ministers of God's truth. This truth can change both your personal life and your ministry.

The promise is that if we are careful about what we hear and we meditate on it, consider it and ponder on it, then virtue and knowledge will come back to us as a result.

Here it is again:

> *The measure [of thought and study] you give [to the truth you hear] will be the measure [of virtue and knowledge] that comes back to you.*

Most of us know what *knowledge* is, but do we truly understand what *virtue* is? What is virtue? According to *Strong's Concordance*, *virtue* means "strength." Virtue empowers you and strengthens you to do exploits.

Virtue means "moral excellence."

Virtue means "a beneficial quality or power." The beneficial qualities and powers we seek are through God's giftings and the anointing, to make us more effective for ministry to those around us. Some of us are called to evangelize, some are gifted prophetically, and some are gifted as teachers. Whatever your giftings are, the Lord will increase them with beneficial qualities and powers.

Virtue means "a commendable quality or trait, merit, courage, valor or potency." God wants to release a new potency (power) into our personal lives and into our ministries.

Virtue means "conformity to a standard of right competency, as if coming into your season." In other words, you will conform to a standard of being capable in all things concerning God's Word, and you will look like you have stepped into your season. In other words, you will speak the Word of God with great power, and those who hear you will know that your season has come.

When we read the Word of God, we often take it at surface value. It might be too much to try to figure out exactly what God is saying, so we often just don't bother trying. Hearing the Word read or spoken or reading it is enough for some, but that's clearly *not* enough. God requires much more. He requires an open heart, a heart that latches on to each truth, meditates on it and makes it their own.

This could be your season, but you will determine if it is or not. This *can be* your season—if you will grasp what God is saying to you and act upon it.

Study and be eager and do your utmost to present yourself to God approved (tested by trial), a

WE ARE ABOUT TO
SEE THE GREATEST
THINGS WE HAVE EVER
EXPERIENCED IN OUR
LIFETIMES!

*workman who has no cause to be ashamed, cor-
rectly analyzing and accurately dividing [rightly
handling and skillfully teaching] the Word of
Truth.*   2 Timothy 2:15

We have seen marvelous things over the past
years, things we could never have dreamed of,
but I am convinced that what we are walking
into now is the greatest of times and the greatest
of opportunities for each and every one of us. We
are about to see the greatest things we have ever
experienced in our lifetimes. Get ready for it. *"Be
careful what you are hearing!"*

"Give Attention to This!"

Give attention to this!   Mark 4:3

Now, let's go back to the earlier portion of Mark 4. Notice that Jesus began His teaching to the disciples with the words: *"Give attention to this!"* This phrase is followed by a strong exclamation point. The King James Version uses the strong word *HEARKEN*! What Jesus was about to say was so important that He had to get the full attention of His disciples. Jesus was saying, "Listen to this!" He was about to reveal to them how the Kingdom of God works.

The Kingdom of God was described by Paul to the believers at Rome as: *"righteousness, peace and joy in the Holy Ghost"* (Romans 14:17, KJV). If we stay in the Kingdom, we reap Kingdom benefits, but we have the ability, at any moment, to step out of the boundaries of God's Kingdom onto what I call "foreign soil," in other words, sin. When we do this, we forfeit our Kingdom rights. I need God's righteousness, His peace and His joy. So, I must stay within the boundaries of His Kingdom.

Once Jesus had the disciples' full attention He began His teaching:

Behold, a sower went out to sow.   Mark 4:3

If we can comprehend it, there is a world of meaning in those words. Who is *"the sower"*? First of all, of course, He is Jesus through the Holy Spirit. He sows His Word in us. We might call Him the Master Sower. But, just as the disciples of Jesus emulated Him and became sowers of the seed, we, too, are called to become sowers of His seed in our world and in our time.

In everything that we do as believers, we are sowing seeds. When we pray and intercede for others, we are sowing seeds that will surely reap a great harvest. When we testify of God's goodness, we are sowing seeds that will bear fruit in others. When we give to God, we are sowing seeds that will surely come back to us in *"good*

WE HAVE THE ABILITY,
AT ANY MOMENT,
TO STEP OUT OF THE
BOUNDARIES OF GOD'S
KINGDOM ONTO WHAT
I CALL "FOREIGN SOIL,"
IN OTHER WORDS, SIN.
WHEN WE DO THIS, WE
FORFEIT OUR KINGDOM
RIGHTS!

measure, pressed down, and shaken together and running over" (Luke 6:38, KJV).

The Scriptures clearly teach:

Do not be deceived and deluded and misled; ... whatever a man sows, that and that only is what he will reap.   Galatians 6:7

[Remember] this: he who sows sparingly and grudgingly will also reap sparingly and grudgingly, and he who sows generously [that blessings may come to someone] will also reap generously and with blessings.
                                 2 Corinthians 9:6

I wish I could be there by your side today pouring seeds on you as you read these words, to illustrate the fact that the Holy Spirit is forever lavishing each of us with His wonderful seeds. Don't ignore them. Don't shove them aside. Embrace them, and let them grow and produce their intended harvest.

Even as you read this book, the words of it are filled with Kingdom seed that is being sown into your heart, your mind and your spirit man. *Give attention to this.*

PART II

Understanding the
Power of a Seed

CHAPTER 4

Putting Something into Motion

Then Isaac sowed seed in that land and received in the same year a hundred times as much as he had planted, and the LORD favored him with blessings. And the man became great and gained more and more until he became very wealthy and distinguished; he owned flocks, herds, and a great supply of servants, and the Philistines envied him.   Genesis 26:12-14

This word *sow* means more than just placing a seed in the ground. Another meaning is "to put something into motion." Isn't that interesting!

Every time a seed is sown, something is being put into motion. When you take your tithes and offerings to the House of God and place them into the offering receptacle, something is put into motion at that very instant. You may not see the results immediately, but the seed has been planted, and there WILL be a harvest. It's guaranteed.

This truth goes far beyond tithing and giving. When you sow seeds of kindness in any way, something is put into motion. Of course, if the seed you sow is evil, that, too, will reap a harvest, an evil harvest. When you speak a word of prophecy to others, that seed will bear good fruit.

When you are preaching or teaching the Word of God, you are sowing seeds, marvelous seeds, into the hearts and lives of the people you are ministering to. There have been times, when I was preaching the Word, that I could literally see hundreds and thousands of seeds falling into the hearts and lives of the people I was ministering to, and I knew that a harvest, a fruitful harvest, would indeed come forth.

Again, the Master Sower sows seeds in you. Why? His desire is that you prosper and move forward in His Kingdom. Even now, there is seed being sown into your life through the words of this book. Let them work in you to produce the desired harvest. Start putting something into motion.

THIS TRUTH GOES FAR
BEYOND TITHING AND
GIVING. WHEN YOU SOW
SEEDS OF KINDNESS IN
ANY WAY, SOMETHING IS
PUT INTO MOTION!

CHAPTER 5

Becoming Fruitful

Then Isaac sowed seed in that land and received in the same year a hundred times as much as he had planted. Genesis 26:12

Another meaning for the word *sow*, according to *Strong's*, is "to be fructified." *Fructified* is not a word that we commonly use in everyday English, but it's a great word with a great meaning. This is a process that happens to you to make you fruitful. How many are ready to be fructified?

As a verb used with an object, *fructify* means "to bear fruit; become fruitful." As a verb without an object, it means "to make fruitful or productive; fertilize." Either way, it's a wonderful process with a wonderful outcome.

This means that suddenly fruitfulness is springing up on the inside of you. Your action of sowing fructifies you. Every time you sow a seed of any kind, you are being fructified. This is an immediate action that takes place in your life. The moment you sow a seed, fruitfulness begins to explode in your life.

Fructify also means "to bear fruit, to make fruitful or productive." You are being made fruitful, and you are being made productive. Here again, the process of being fruitful is immediately apparent.

I can see by the Spirit that the Lord of the Harvest is taking up seed and casting it over *you* even now. He is scattering it skillfully in the soil of your spirit, and if you allow it to germinate and grow, something wonderful will surely result.

The seeds the Master Sower is sowing in you are seeds of greatness, seeds of joy, seeds of blessing and seeds of financial provision. There are also seeds of ministry, seeds of prophetic ability and seeds of teaching ability. He is lavishing these upon you even now. Receive them and expect your corresponding harvest.

FRUCTIFY ALSO MEANS "TO BEAR FRUIT, TO MAKE FRUITFUL OR PRODUCTIVE." YOU ARE BEING MADE FRUITFUL, AND YOU ARE BEING MADE PRODUCTIVE!

CHAPTER 6

Conceiving

Then Isaac sowed seed in that land and received
in the same year a hundred times as much as he
had planted.   Genesis 26:12

Another meaning of the word *sow*, according
to *Strong's*, is "to conceive." The moment you
sow your seed—your tithes, your offering, or the
Word of God, as you are preaching or teaching
it—something immediately begins to happen.
A conception takes place. Something is being
birthed on the inside of you that was not there
before. It has already been set into motion, and
you will receive a harvest, whether it is in your
finances, the reaping of the goodness of God, or
seeing fruit come forth because of your preaching or teaching of the Word. This harvest will be

for your own life and also for the lives of those you minister to. When you sow seed, you begin to conceive something from the Holy Spirit. You are impregnated with goodness.

Conceive in this context actually means "to conceive knowledge." You might conceive ideas, purposes or plans.

You may not even be aware of this conception taking place, but God is doing it. He gives you what *Webster's* calls "the capacity to function or process of forming or understanding ideas." How many of you would like for God to add knowledge to you that you did not have before?

Every time you sow your seed, something marvelous immediately begins to happen in your life that will take you on a great journey of life and ministry. Start conceiving!

GOD IS DOING IT.
HE GIVES YOU WHAT
WEBSTER'S CALLS "THE
CAPACITY TO FUNCTION
OR PROCESS OF FORMING
OR UNDERSTANDING
IDEAS!"

CHAPTER 7

Disseminating

*Then Isaac sowed seed in that land and received
in the same year a hundred times as much as he
had planted.* Genesis 26:12

Another meaning of the word *sow,* according to
Strong's, is "disseminate." Dissemination has to
do with spreading or giving out knowledge or in-
formation. Sowing produces a dissemination that
can bless many others. When you conceive knowledge, you are then given the ability to spread that
knowledge abroad, giving out or disseminating
the knowledge you have conceived.

When you sow your finances or the Word of
God, a process known as dissemination is immediately put into effect in your life. Knowledge
you did not have before you sowed will begin to

flow, and you will spread this knowledge abroad, giving out knowledge you did not know or understand before. Don't you love God's Kingdom and how it works? The Kingdom of Heaven is creative, constantly propelling us forward. Start disseminating today.

DON'T YOU LOVE GOD'S KINGDOM AND HOW IT WORKS? THE KINGDOM OF HEAVEN IS CREATIVE, CONSTANTLY PROPELLING US FORWARD!

CHAPTER 8

Producing Growth and Development

And other seed [of the same kind] fell into good (well-adapted) soil and brought forth grain, growing up and increasing, and yielded up to thirty times as much, and sixty times as much, and even a hundred times as much as had been sown. Mark 4:8

Another meaning of the word *seed* is "to furnish with something that stimulates growth and development." By the Spirit and through faith in the Word of God, the Lord of the Harvest is about to stimulate growth and development in you. The seeds being dropped into your spirit are putting something into motion, and are stimulating something in your life that causes growth and development.

There are ministries in you that God wants to release. There are powerful seeds in you that need to be developed. Maybe you need to be preaching the Word, or you need to be teaching or prophesying. Something is being put into motion in your life, and it will stimulate growth and development.

I'm so glad that God is in control of the seed and its destiny. You and I could never do such great things, but to Him, they are easy.

Jesus taught that a seed must go into the ground and die so that life can come forth from it:

> *I assure you, most solemnly I tell you, Unless a grain of wheat falls into the earth and dies, it remains [just one grain; it never becomes more but lives] by itself alone. But if it dies, it produces many others and yields a rich harvest.*
> John 12:24

The death of that seed results in a brand new plant springing forth and ultimately bringing forth fruit. Let that be your testimony.

Far too many of us go to church these days simply out of Christian duty, and we may be

I'M SO GLAD THAT GOD
IS IN CONTROL OF THE
SEED AND ITS DESTINY.
YOU AND I COULD NEVER
DO SUCH GREAT THINGS,
BUT TO HIM, THEY ARE
EASY!

surprised by what God has just waiting for us. We might just stumble into something wonderful as His seeds are planted in our spirit. You may be crossing over a threshold, and nothing will be the same from this moment on. Seeds bring growth and development. Let it happen in you and through you.

CHAPTER 9

What God Can Do with a Seed

But someone will say, How can the dead be raised? With what [kind of] body will they come forth? You foolish man! Every time you plant seed, you sow something that does not come to life [germinating, springing up, and growing] unless it dies first. Nor is the seed you sow then the body which it is going to have [later], but it is a naked kernel, perhaps of wheat or some of the rest of the grains. But God gives to it the body that He plans and sees fit, and to each kind of seed a body of its own.

1 Corinthians 15:35-38

We have already established that in order for a seed to produce, it must go into the ground and die. That seed is *"naked"* and outwardly appears to have very little value, but the full potential is in there. In the same way, in the Spirit realm, we know that we must first die in order to really live.

"With what [kind of] body will they come forth?" Paul asked. Before long, your seed will sprout, and you will come forth as a totally new person. Then you will no longer act the same or talk the same.

These are good questions that Paul was asking. How can a dead person live again? And what kind of body will they have? The answer he came up with was this:

> *Every time you plant seed, you sow something that does not come to life [germinating, springing up, and growing] unless it dies first.*
>
> Verse 36

God, the Mater Sower, has put something into motion in our lives. It will bring forth growth and development. As you get yourself planted in good soil, the results will amaze even *you*. When you go into the ground, you may not seem to have great potential, but when your seed germinates and brings forth a plant and then its fruit, everyone will see it and know what a miracle it is.

BEFORE LONG, YOUR SEED WILL SPROUT, AND YOU WILL COME FORTH AS A TOTALLY NEW PERSON!

Nor is the seed you sow then the body which it is going to have [later], but it is a naked kernel, perhaps of wheat or some of the rest of the grains.
                                                        Verse 37

Again, every seed is just what Paul described, a naked kernel. Could you take such a small and insignificant thing and make it into something wonderful? Surely not, but God can:

But God gives to it the body that He plans and sees fit, and to each kind of seed a body of its own.   Verse 38

Again, you are a seed. If you can get planted in the right kind of soil, God will do His wonders in you, and the result will be something of favor, blessing and greatness. And if you can sow your seed in good soil, the same will be true.

Is your faith rising? Are you believing God for the needed miracle? Something has been put into motion in your spirit that will produce growth and development. Protect it and allow it to grow, and you will be amazed by the result.

If you have ever planted any seeds, you know what happens next. At first, nothing seems to be happening, for the seed takes a little time to germinate. This varies from seed to seed. But if the soil is right, the temperature is right and the rainfall or irrigation is right, you are guaranteed a harvest. Before long, a new plant will push its way through the soil and begin to reach heavenward.

That resulting plant and the fruit it will eventually produce looks nothing like the seed it came from. This is something new, something miraculous, something that only God could do. But He does it so consistently that farmers around the world can count on it. They sow with great expectation, for seeds do not fail. God stands behind His creation and guarantees its success.

As you are sown and die to self, God begins His work. He gives you a body (and all the rest) as it suits Him, but what He gives you is always good and always for your benefit.

When the children of Israel came out of Egypt, they were not very impressive. They were just coming out of slavery. But God told them that if they would stick with Him through the wilderness and be faithful, when they eventually marched into the Promised Land, they would do so as a kingdom of distinguished priests. And that's exactly what happened. Be assured that God has greatness in mind for you too.

WHAT PAUL HAS WRITTEN HERE MAY WELL REFER TO THE END-TIMES, WHEN THE DEAD IN CHRIST WILL BE RAISED AND THEIR PHYSICAL BODIES WILL BE TRANSFORMED, BUT IT MEANS SOMETHING MORE THAN THAT TO US WHO ARE STILL HERE!

What God Can Do with a Seed

Now, let's look at Paul's questions again: *"How can the dead be raised?"* he asked. Did you perhaps feel dead when you started reading this book? Know that your dead seed can produce incredible life.

"With what [kind of] body will they come forth?" What Paul has written here may well refer to the end-times, when the dead in Christ will be raised and their physical bodies will be transformed, but it means something more than that to us who are still here. He said:

> *You foolish man! Every time you plant seed, you sow something that does not come to life [germinating, springing up, and growing] unless it dies first.*   1 Corinthians 15:36

Again, we know that a seed must first die before it can bring forth new life. If you haven't yet experienced that miracle of death and rebirth, get ready. Paul continued:

> *Nor is the seed you sow then the body which it is going to have [later], but it is a naked kernel, perhaps of wheat or some of the rest of the grains.*   1 Corinthians 15:37

We need to get excited about our potential. We have sown a seed, seeds have been sown in us, and now we can expect to see what fruit they will produce.

Surely that fruit will amaze us all. The seed has a certain look when it is sown, but when a harvest is produced from it, that harvest is something wonderfully different.

Paul continued:

> *But God gives to it the body that He plans and sees fit, and to each kind of seed a body of its own.* 1 Corinthians 15:38

God gives us the body He has planned and sees fit. For each of us, this represents a mighty transformation that is about to take place in us. If you put your seed in the ground, you will soon not even resemble that seed.

When a new mantle comes upon you and an office is executed over you, suddenly people will not believe who you have become. They will hardly be able to believe where you came from and what all God has done on your behalf. That transformation has already started. Your seed is germinating and is about to pop through the soil, and when it happens, you will no longer be the same.

THE SEED HAS A
CERTAIN LOOK WHEN IT
IS SOWN, BUT WHEN A
HARVEST IS PRODUCED
FROM IT, THAT HARVEST
IS SOMETHING
WONDERFULLY
DIFFERENT!

When God made a covenant with Abraham, Isaac, and Jacob, He had a plan. When Jacob and his descendants went into Egypt and lived in bondage to the pharaohs for 452 years, God raised up a deliverer for them. Their lives, at that point, seemed chaotic, but in the language of our day, God said to them:

> Hang in there with Me. You will go through bitterness, but My glory will be there in the midst of it all, and I will carry you past every obstacle and on into the Promised Land. If you will just hang in there with Me, I promise you that when you march into that blessed land, you will not look the same. You have come out of Egypt as slaves, but you will march into the land as a kingdom of priests, totally changed for My glory.

As the people of Israel came out of Egypt, they may not have made a very good impression. However, forty years later they would march into the Promised Land clothed as royalty. In the same way, God is now changing your garments and making all things new.

God will do it, not you. He does it for His glory. You could do nothing to make it happen. Only

God could do this. Be pliable in His hands, and let Him mold you as He desires. There is no limit to what God can do with a seed.

AS THE PEOPLE OF
ISRAEL CAME OUT OF
EGYPT, THEY MAY NOT
HAVE MADE A VERY
GOOD IMPRESSION. BUT
FORTY YEARS LATER
THEY WOULD MARCH
INTO THE PROMISED
LAND CLOTHED AS
ROYALTY!

CHAPTER **10**

The Importance of the Condition of the Soil

Behold, a sower went out to sow.   Mark 4:3

Next, in the Parable of the Sower and the Seed, Jesus presented us with four very different scenarios related to the seed and how well it produces (or not), depending on the soil it was sown into. The first of those scenarios was this:

And as he was sowing, some seed fell along the path, and the birds came and ate it up.   Mark 4:4

The second scenario was this:

Other seed [of the same kind] fell on ground full

77

of rocks, where it had not much soil; and at once it sprang up, because it had no depth of soil; and when the sun came up, it was scorched, and because it had not taken root, it withered away.
Mark 4:5-6

The third scenario was this:

Other seed [of the same kind] fell among thorn plants, and the thistles grew and pressed together and utterly choked and suffocated it, and it yielded no grain.
Mark 4:7

The fourth scenario is the good one, the one we all want:

And other seed [of the same kind] fell into good (well-adapted) soil and brought forth grain, growing up and increasing, and yielded up to thirty times as much, and sixty times as much, and even a hundred times as much as had been sown.
Mark 4:8

The various types of bad soil can refer to difficult situations or sometimes to places. The *thorns* and *weeds* Jesus spoke of represent the constant thoughts of greed and wrong motives present in

THE VARIOUS TYPES OF BAD SOIL CAN REFER TO DIFFICULT SITUATIONS OR SOMETIMES TO PLACES!

some situations. You cannot afford to stay in that condition very long, for there you cannot and will not grow or prosper.

Are you being adversely affected by stoney ground? Is your heart hardened because of situations or circumstances? Does it need to be circumcised? Let God come and roll away all reproach from you. He moves in hearts of flesh, hearts that are soft and pliable in His hands. Ask the Lord to show you your need in this regard.

If you belong to a church that is not fertile soil, your seed will be adversely affected. Are you sowing into soil that can bring forth life?

Get into some good soil. Get planted in a place where Judah (praise) breaks up the fallow ground and prepares the soil well for optimum results. Find yourself a church home where the gifts of the Spirit are operating and where revelation knowledge is flowing. That's the kind of soil that will do your seed the most good.

The Master Sower is even now sowing seeds over us, but it is up to us to be sure that we are planted where we can thrive.

Also make sure that you sow your own seed into good ground. When you sow, you are setting something into motion, something that Satan wants to stop but cannot if the soil is properly tilled through praise and the Word of God. Then seed can be sown and will bring forth a harvest.

A little later in this fourth chapter of Mark, Jesus explained what He meant by the birds that came and ate the seed in verse 4. He said that it was Satan himself who came to devour the seed. Satan will do his best to pluck up what God has sown in your life.

Those stones in verse 5 may represent the condition of your heart. Stoney ground, a stoney heart, will not leave room for a spiritual plant to develop as it should. That was why David prayed to God:

> *Create in me a clean heart, O God, and renew a right, persevering, and steadfast spirit within me.*   Psalm 51:10

A seed is powerful, and it will germinate and spring up almost anywhere. But if it is not planted deeply enough in the soil or the soil is not good for planting, that seed cannot become fruitful. In fact, the resulting sprout will probably die when the sun gets hot enough. In order to grow until it produces fruit, a seed requires deep soil.

Do you ever feel *"choked"* or *"suffocated"* so that you cannot bear fruit? You may be suffering from

SEEDS PLANTED IN
GOOD GROUND DO
AMAZING THINGS. THEY
CAN PRODUCE *"THIRTY
TIMES AS MUCH,"* OR
"SIXTY TIMES AS MUCH,"
AND, AMAZINGLY, *"EVEN
A HUNDRED TIMES AS
MUCH"* AS HAS BEEN
SOWN!

the thorns and thistles that are planted to work against you.

Seeds planted in good ground do amazing things. They can produce *"thirty times as much,"* or *"sixty times as much,"* and, amazingly, *"even a hundred times as much"* as has been sown. That's what you want, and now you know how to get it. Get your seed planted in the proper soil of your life and watch it grow and produce an abundant harvest.

CHAPTER 11

The Certainty of the Harvest

While the earth remains, seedtime and harvest, cold and heat, summer and winter, and day and night shall not cease. Genesis 8:22

After the Great Flood, God assured mankind that the seasons would come and go normally from then on. Winter would invariably turn into spring, spring would give way to summer, summer would yield to fall, and fall would lead us into another winter.

And something else would be consistent— *"seedtime and harvest."* These seasons, God said, *"shall not cease."* In other words, seedtime and harvest are constant, sure and unfailing.

Now, it's not always summer, and it's not always winter, but it is always seedtime somewhere, and it is always time for a harvest somewhere. It is always time to sow something, and it is always time to reap something.

As we have seen, to sow means "to put something into motion." This is important to understand because every day of our lives and every moment of those days we are sowing some kind of seed. As we have seen, at the same time, the great Sower of the Universe is sowing into our lives every moment of every day. We may not be aware of it, but there are seeds constantly being dropped on us, and each one of them sets something into motion.

When we sow, something is conceived, and something is set in motion that will produce growth and development. The minute you sow, you become fruitful, you are fructified, you begin to take in supernatural knowledge. This, Jesus taught, is how the Kingdom of God operates. He emphasized:

Do you not discern and understand this parable? How then is it possible for you to discern and understand all the parables?   Mark 4:13

This parable is important, and we need to understand it.

WE MAY NOT BE AWARE
OF IT, BUT THERE ARE
SEEDS CONSTANTLY
BEING DROPPED ON US,
AND EACH ONE OF THEM
SETS SOMETHING INTO
MOTION!

As we have seen, to *sow* means "to cause growth and development." Seeds are falling upon us on a regular basis, and when it happens, something is being set into motion, and that seed is causing growth and development. It is happening right now.

I decree over you even now that you must *"arise and shine"* for your season has come. Isaiah declared it:

> *Arise, shine; for thy light is come, and the glory of the* Lord *is risen upon thee.*   Isaiah 60:1, KJV

The Classic Version of the Amplified Bible says it this way:

> *Arise [from the depression and prostration in which circumstances have kept you—rise to a new life]! Shine (be radiant with the glory of the* Lord*), for your light has come, and the glory of the* Lord *has risen upon you!*

Why should we arise? Because our season has come. You may not have seen the fullness of it until now, but it's here. Embrace it.

PART III

Understanding the Enemy's Plot Against the Seed

CHAPTER 12

The Thief of Your Seed

As He was still speaking, Judas, one of the Twelve [apostles], came up, and with him a great crowd with swords and clubs, from the chief priests and elders of the people. Now the betrayer had given them a sign, saying, The One I shall kiss is the Man; seize Him. And he came up to Jesus at once and said, Hail (greetings, good health to You, long life to You), Master! And he embraced Him and kissed Him with [pretended] warmth and devotion. Matthew 26:47-49

Then Herod, when he realized that he had been misled by the wise men, was furiously enraged, and he sent and put to death all the male children in Bethlehem and in all that territory who were two years old and under, reckoning according to the date which he had investigated diligently and had learned exactly from the wise men. Matthew 2:16

Then the king of Egypt said to the Hebrew mid-wives, of whom one was named Shiprah and the other Puah, When you act as midwives to the Hebrew women and see them on the birthstool, if it is a son, you shall kill him; but if it is a daughter, she shall live. Exodus 1:15-16

The plot of Judas, the plot of Hitler, the plot of Herod, the plot of the Pharaoh and the plot of Haman to annihilate the Jews of Esther's time all had the same author. It was Satan, the great Anti-Christ, operating through each of them. His motivation was the thought that if he could kill the seed, he would stop the move of God. While you are determined to sow your seed and reap a great harvest, the enemy is plotting against you. And his plot is still the same today. He wants to kill you and your seed.

You need to understand this, for every time something wonderful happens to you, the enemy comes and tries to steal it away, telling you that you were mistaken. It never happened. If this is allowed to continue, you will never reach the level God has destined for you. Somehow you must overcome the thief of your seed.

EVERY TIME SOMETHING WONDERFUL HAPPENS TO YOU, THE ENEMY COMES AND TRIES TO STEAL IT AWAY, TELLING YOU THAT YOU WERE MISTAKEN!

When Herod ordered the death of all Jewish boy babies two years old and under, he was being inspired by Satan himself. Herod may have been thinking he was preserving his own throne (since some were calling Jesus *"the King of the Jews"*). If he could just kill that Seed, his throne would be safe. Behind the plot, however, was Satan, intent on destroying the Christ before He could become active and work to pull down the evil kingdoms of this world.

Later, when men again tried to kill Jesus, they seemed to have succeeded. But we know now that the seed in Him could not be extinguished. He overcame, conquering death, Hell and the grave. And that is a word for you today. Your seed cannot be killed either. No weapon formed against you will prosper. (We'll see this more in detail in the following chapter.)

In Exodus 1, a mighty shift began in the earth. Four hundred and fifty some years before, God had made covenant with Abraham, promising him that his seed and his seed's seed would inherit the earth. That's a long time to wait for the fulfillment of a promise.

In time, Jacob (Abraham's grandson) and Jacob's sons and grandchildren, seventy people in all, moved to Egypt because of a severe famine. As the years passed, they all died there in Egypt. Four hundred and fifty some years later, when a different Pharaoh was ruling, God was ready to bring their descendants out and take them into their Promised Land. Their season had come, and a serious paradigm shift was about to take place.

It was to be another forty years before they could reach the land, and that, too, is a long time to wait. Thank God He has promised that in the end of time, the days will be shortened for the elect's sake (see Matthew 24:22).

The story found in Exodus is true, and it really happened. But, at the same time, it is an allegory, a type and shadow for us to follow today. The story goes like this:

> *These are the names of the sons of Israel who came into Egypt with Jacob, each with his household: Reuben, Simeon, Levi, and Judah, Issachar, Zebulun, and Benjamin, Dan and Naphtali, Gad and Asher. All the offspring of Jacob were seventy persons; Joseph was already in Egypt.*
> *Then Joseph died, and all his brothers and all that generation. But the descendants of Israel were fruitful and increased abundantly; they multiplied and grew exceedingly strong, and the land was full of them.*   Exodus 1:1-7

"THE DESCENDANTS OF ISRAEL WERE FRUITFUL AND INCREASED ABUNDANTLY." WHY? BECAUSE THE SEED OF CHRIST WAS IN THEM!

The sons of Israel (originally Jacob) who are named here became the various tribes of Israel, and they were the seed (or descendants) of Abraham. For his part, Abraham had two sons — Isaac and Ishmael. Isaac received the promised blessing of Abraham.

Isaac had two sons — Jacob and Esau. Esau sold his birthright for a bowl of pottage, and so Jacob received the promise. The sons of Jacob then gave birth to the various tribes of Israel.

"The descendants of Israel were fruitful and increased abundantly." Why? Because the seed of Christ was in them. Therefore the current Pharaoh hated them, for He was jealous of God's people:

> *Now a new king arose over Egypt who did not know Joseph. He said to his people, Behold, the Israelites are too many and too mighty for us [and they outnumber us both in people and in strength]. Come, let us deal shrewdly with them, lest they multiply more and, should war befall us, they join our enemies, fight against us, and escape out of the land. So they set over [the Israelites] taskmasters to afflict and oppress them with [increased] burdens. And [the Israelites] built Pithom and Rameses as store cities for Pharaoh.* Exodus 1:8-11

In spite of this harsh treatment, God's people continued to prosper, and this provoked an even more cruel response from the Pharaoh:

But the more [the Egyptians] oppressed them, the more they multiplied and expanded, so that [the Egyptians] were vexed and alarmed because of the Israelites. And the Egyptians reduced the Israelites to severe slavery. They made their lives bitter with hard service in mortar, brick, and all kinds of work in the field. All their service was with harshness and severity.

Exodus 1:11-14

As if all of this was not enough, now Pharaoh resorted to murder as a tool of mastery:

Then the king of Egypt said to the Hebrew midwives, of whom one was named Shiprah and the other Puah, when you act as midwives to the Hebrew women and see them on the birthstool, if it is a son, you shall kill him; but if it is a daughter, she shall live.   Exodus 1:15-16

Killing all the boy babies seemed like a logical way to reduce the strength of the Israelites and to hinder any further expansion on their part. It

"BUT THE MORE [THE EGYPTIANS] OPPRESSED THEM, THE MORE THEY MULTIPLIED AND EXPANDED, SO THAT [THE EGYPTIANS] WERE VEXED AND ALARMED BECAUSE OF THE ISRAELITES!"

didn't work because those two women feared God more than they feared man:

> *But the midwives feared God and did not do as the king of Egypt commanded, but let the male babies live.*
> *So the king of Egypt called for the midwives and said to them, Why have you done this thing and allowed the male children to live?*
> *The midwives answered Pharaoh, Because the Hebrew women are not like the Egyptian women; they are vigorous and quickly delivered; their babies are born before the midwife comes to them.*
> *So God dealt well with the midwives and the people multiplied and became very strong.*
>
> Exodus 1:17-20

The nation of Israel was at a threshold, and the spirit of Pharaoh, the same spirit that is in the world today, came against them, trying to hinder their growth and prosperity. But God had predestined this nation of slaves to rise up and become a nation of priests and worshippers, an example to the rest of the world.

This terrible spirit that drove the Pharaoh to abuse the children of God is yet alive in the earth today, and those of us who love God have felt its wrath. The life of the Israelites in captivity was so harsh that it caused bitterness to rise in some of them, but the truth was that God still had great plans for them.

Each time God was about to bring a great shift in the earth, the enemy rose up to try to stop it. Moses' birth signaled that a great shift was coming, and the enemy recognized it and tried to stop it.

"Kill every son," the Pharaoh ordered, and he thought this act of violence would do the job of reducing the strength of the people of God. Killing the seed would stop the move of God. It would stop the paradigm shift. It would stop the plan of God. Killing the seed would prevent this nation of people, who were quickly gaining strength, from crossing over the threshold and receiving all that God had for them. "Kill the seed!" Pharaoh boldly decreed.

The very same thing happened when Jesus was born. Herod, fearing competition for his throne, sent his soldiers to kill all the boy babies two years old and under.

"Kill the seed!"

"Kill the firstborn!"

"Kill the seed, and there will be no move of God."

Over and over again, this has been the tactic of the enemy: "Kill the seed!"

BELOVED, IF YOU ARE IN THE KINGDOM OF GOD AND THE SEED OF CHRIST IS IN YOU, YOU ARE NOW THE ONE ON THE BIRTHING STOOL, AND THE ENEMY IS INTENT UPON KILLING THE SEED IN YOU!

The Pharaoh appealed to the midwives to help him in this mission. "When you see them on the birthing stool and it's a son, kill him," he told them.

Beloved, if you are in the Kingdom of God and the seed of Christ is in you, you are now the one on the birthing stool, and the enemy is intent upon killing the seed in you.

The birthing stool spoken of here was a literal stool used for giving birth to babies, but the phrase used to describe it also means "a potter's wheel." "When you see them on the potter's wheel, kill them." If you are on the Potter's wheel, it must mean that you are in the Kingdom of God, and He is shaping you into the vessel He desires for you to be. Satan will do anything to stop that work.

This word for *son* also meant "builder." "When you see a builder, kill him. Kill the seed!"

A son being born also spoke of obtaining children. "When you see someone obtaining children [we're speaking of the spiritual now], kill them." When the enemy sees that the Lord is adding to you spiritual sons and daughters, his plot is to kill your seed. "When you see them increasing, kill them."

This word also referred to repairing something. "When you see them repairing something in the Kingdom, kill them."

The word also referred to a plummet. Since most of us don't use a plummet, perhaps we need a definition. Dictionary.com defines *plummet* as "Also called plumb bob, a piece of lead or some other weight attached to a line, used for determining perpendicularity, for sounding, etc.; the bob of a plumb line." Before modern tools were available, a plummet was used to determine the "plumb" or vertical straightness that had to be determined before anything was built. "When you see them with a plummet in their hands, beginning to build, kill them," Satan decreed. "Kill the seed."

This word also spoke of being "in position." "When you see them in position, kill them." God is putting you into position for ministry, and the enemy will do all that he can to stop you.

In ancient times, having a son was very different from having a daughter. The firstborn son carried the inheritance of the entire family. This word *son* meant "a builder of the family." "When you see a builder of the family," Satan was saying, "kill him." I'm sure that you are called to be a builder of the family of God, so be alert, for the enemy has plans to stop

GOD IS PUTTING YOU INTO POSITION FOR MINISTRY, AND THE ENEMY WILL DO ALL THAT HE CAN TO STOP YOU!

you, hinder you or prevent you from being successful.

The Scriptures teach us:

Not forsaking or neglecting to assemble together [as believers], as is the habit of some people, but admonishing (warning, urging, and encouraging) one another, and all the more faithfully as you see the day approaching. Hebrews 10:25

We need the strength of each other to fight this battle.

This word *son* was also used to denote "a nation rising." "When you see a nation rising, kill it." This is Satan's intent, but thank God, we have His promise:

No weapon that is formed against you will prosper. Isaiah 54:17

Beware of the thief who is intent upon stealing your seed.

CHAPTER 13

The Enemy's Attempt to Destroy the Seed

No weapon that is formed against you shall prosper.   Isaiah 54:17

It has always been noted that if you kill a seed, you stop its potential to produce. The enemies of God's people understood this principle and thought that if they could kill the seed of Christ, they could stop the move of God. If they could kill the seed of the Jewish people, they could prevent God from further blessing them. But God said that no weapon formed against us will prosper.

This is God's promise given through the prophet Isaiah. That's not to say that a weapon will not be formed against you. It *will* be formed, and you may see it being formed. You may even see it being launched against you. The promise it that any and all weapons formed against you will not prosper. We can be thankful for that assurance. The seed will prevail.

To understand this fully, we need to look to the story of Queen Esther. In her time, there was an evil man named Haman who had befriended the king. Haman, however, operated in the same spirit that moved Judas, the same spirit that was in Hitler, the same spirit that was in Herod in Jesus' day and the same spirit that was in the Pharaoh of Egypt in Moses' day. Haman hated the Jewish people and set about to find a way to destroy them.

Again, this spirit is still alive in the world today, and the proof is that there are those who dedicate their lives to destroying Israel and the Jewish people, and there are also those who live to destroy Christians wherever they are found. This hatred is nothing new.

When Esther learned of Haman's plot, she knew that she had to do something about it. By law, she was prohibited from entering the king's presence without him having called for her, but she sensed that she had to lay her life on the line to save her people. Famously, she said:

HAMAN OPERATED IN
THE SAME SPIRIT THAT
WAS IN JUDAS, THE SAME
SPIRIT THAT WAS IN
HITLER, THE SAME SPIRIT
THAT WAS IN HEROD
IN JESUS' DAY AND THE
SAME SPIRIT THAT WAS
IN THE PHARAOH OF
EGYPT IN MOSES' DAY!

I will go to the king, though it is against the law;
and if I perish, I perish.   Esther 4:16

Esther went forth to do her sacred duty.
Thank God that He is raising up some Esthers
in the earth today, those who will risk all to
intercede for God's people, whatever the price.

When Esther went before the king, he was not
angry with her. She found favor in his sight,
and he asked her what she wanted. She didn't
answer right then, but asked him to come to a
dinner the next night and to bring his advisor,
Haman, with him. The king consented.

When Haman heard this, he was elated. He
was about to have a private dinner with the
king and his queen. He couldn't wait to tell his
wife about being invited to dine with the royal
couple. His excitement grew when he and the
king were invited back for a second evening
in the queen's presence. He could hardly wait.
The Scriptures record:

Haman went away that day joyful and elated in
heart.   Esther 5:9

On his way home, Haman passed by the gate
and saw Mordecai, Esther's uncle, sitting there.

Mordecai was a wise man, and he recognized the evil in Haman and refused to bow before him. This enraged Haman.

After reaching home, Haman managed to hold himself together long enough to deliver the good news of his special invitation to his wife and friends. However, he could not resist telling them how much it upset him that this man, Mordecai, was so disrespectful to him.

Haman's wife and friends agreed with him that what Mordecai was doing was terrible, and together they came up with a plan to deal with it. Haman should build a gallows and have Mordecai publicly hanged on that gallows. Haman loved this idea and ordered such a gallows to be constructed with all haste.

What transpired at Esther's banquet that next night, however, was very different from what Haman had expected. Esther now exposed Haman's treachery to his face, and the king was suddenly turned against the man who had beguiled him.

Before this, however, something else unexpected had happened. The king was determined to honor Mordecai because the night before he had not slept well. He had asked his servants to bring to him the Chronicles, a record book that was kept of

HAMAN COULD NOT IMAGINE THAT ANYONE WAS MORE WORTHY OF HONOR THAN HIMSELF, SO HE QUICKLY MADE SOME GENEROUS SUGGESTIONS, THINKING OF WHAT HE WOULD WANT FOR HIMSELF!

memorable deeds in the kingdom, and they read to him from the book. As they read, he noticed that Mordecai had saved the kingdom by exposing the treachery of two trusted guardians. (See Chapter 16 for more on this memorable deed.) *"What was done to honor this man?"* the king asked, and the answer was *"nothing"* (Esther 6:3).

Determined to right this wrong, the king asked who was present in the palace who might assist him, and he was told that Haman had just arrived. The truth was that Haman had come to ask the king to have Mordecai hung on the gallows he had prepared for that purpose.

When Haman was brought before him, the king asked:

What shall be done to the man whom the king delights to honor? Esther 6:6

Haman could not imagine that anyone was more worthy of honor than himself, so he quickly made some generous suggestions, thinking of what he would want for himself:

For the man whom the king delights to honor, let royal apparel be brought which the king has worn and the horse which the king has ridden, and a royal crown be set on his head. And let the apparel and the horse be delivered to the hand of one of the king's most noble princes. Let him array the man whom the king delights to honor, and conduct him on horseback through the open square of the city, and proclaim before him, Thus shall it be done to the man whom the king delights to honor.   Esther 6:7-9

The king loved these suggestions and told Haman to carry them out on the man he wanted to honor. When he named the man, however, Haman fell silent. The man the king wanted to honor was none other than Mordecai, the Jew, whom Haman hated.

"Leave out nothing that you have spoken," the king commanded Haman (Esther 6:10). So, what could Haman do? Totally humiliated and steaming with anger, he was forced to pay homage to his enemy, as the king had commanded. Then he crept home and related to his wife and friends all the humiliation that had befallen him.

Little did Haman know that the worst was yet to come. Even as they spoke, the king's attendants came to take Haman to the dinner that Esther had prepared for him.

LITTLE DID HAMAN KNOW THAT THE WORST WAS YET TO COME. EVEN AS THEY SPOKE, THE KING'S ATTENDANTS CAME TO TAKE HAMAN TO THE DINNER THAT ESTHER HAD PREPARED FOR HIM!

One incident, that moment when Mordecai received revelation of the treachery planned against the throne, turned the situation around and caused the Jewish people to be saved. The end result would be that Haman was hung on the very gallows he had prepared for Mordecai. God turned it all around. Didn't He promise?

> *No weapon that is formed against you shall prosper, and every tongue that shall rise against you in judgment you shall show to be in the wrong. This [peace, righteousness, security, triumph over opposition] is the heritage of the servants of the LORD [those in whom the ideal Servant of the LORD is reproduced]; this is the righteousness or the vindication which they obtain from Me [this is that which I impart to them as their justification], says the LORD.*   Isaiah 54:17

The enemy hates the seed of God and will do anything to destroy us, but God has promised that no weapon formed against us will prosper.

CHAPTER 14

Mordecai's Deliverance and Haman's Defeat

In those days, while Mordecai sat in the king's gate, two of the king's chamberlains, Bigthan and Teresh, of those which kept the door, were wroth, and sought to lay hands on the king Ahasuerus.
Esther 2:21

And it was found written, that Mordecai had told of Bigthan and Teresh, two of the king's chamberlains, the keepers of the door, who sought to lay hand on the king Ahasuerus. Esther 6:2

Bible commentaries state that these two men, Bigthan and Teresh, were "guardians of the threshold." As such, they were very important and trusted servants, and so, when they plotted against the king, their treachery was very dangerous for him and also for the entire kingdom.

You need to know that with every threshold that will bring you to advancement in God's Kingdom, there will be evil men waiting to hinder you and do you harm. Just as Paul wrote that with every effectual door given to him, there were many adversaries waiting to try to stop him or, at the very least, to hinder his progress (see 1 Corinthians 16:9).

The story of Queen Esther, found in the book that also bears her name, is true, but it is also an allegory and can teach us many things. Her uncle Mordecai, a type of the Holy Spirit, was honored to sit at the gates of the city (see Esther 2:21). This was a strategic position. The gate was not only an important place of business. It was also there, in the gate, where all political decisions were made. The respected elders of the land met there on a regular basis, and Mordecai was among them.

One of the meanings of the word *gate*, according to *Strong's Concordance*, is "the place of resorting to God for help." Those gates were the threshold to the entire kingdom.

In ancient times, there were eunuchs, also called "king's chamberlains," who were assigned to

ONE OF THE MEANINGS
OF THE WORD
GATE, **ACCORDING
TO** *STRONG'S
CONCORDANCE,* **IS** *"THE
PLACE OF RESORTING TO
GOD FOR HELP!"*

guard the threshold. They became known as "the Guardians of the Threshold." In the time of King Ahasuerus, two of these men, Bigthan and Teresh, for some unknown or unspecified reason, turned against the king and thought to do him harm. This king was a type or shadow of our God, so this was a serious matter.

This evil plot became known to Mordecai because of his activities at the gates, and he saved the king and the kingdom. The treachery of these two men was uncovered, and they were hanged. As noted earlier, a record of this was entered into the official Book of the Chronicles.

Haman's plot to kill the Jewish people was birthed out of this same spirit, the assignment in the earth to kill the seed. Bigthan and Teresh were moved by this same evil spirit. Entrusted with guarding the threshold and preventing the entrance of unwanted enemies, they themselves turned on the king and wanted to stop the seed. If they could kill the seed, they could stop the progress of the kingdom or, literally, annihilate it.

Haman had this same spirit. He wanted to destroy all the Jewish people in the kingdom. He had managed to ingratiate himself with the king, and the king, not realizing what an evil man Haman was, had elevated him above the other princes of the kingdom and ordered all others to bow to him. Like Lucifer, his father, Haman wanted all the glory.

It was revelation knowledge given to Mordecai that saved the day. Now, Haman had a similar plot. I declare that from this day forward, God will enlighten you with revelation, and as the attacks of the enemy come to try to destroy the seed in you, God will give you victory after victory over the evil one. God has already confirmed to you that the seed cannot be killed. It *will* live and produce fruit.

Again, the spirit driving Haman was the same spirit that was in Adolf Hitler when he set about to annihilate the Jews of Europe. It was the same spirit that drove the Pharaoh of Moses' day to have all of the male Jewish babies killed, the same spirit that drove Herod to have all the babies of Jesus' day two years old and under slaughtered, and the same spirit that controlled Judas, when he betrayed Jesus in the Garden of Gethsemane.

This was that same Anti-Christ spirit that crucified Jesus. The enemy thought that if he could just kill Jesus, in other words, kill the Seed, he would kill the plans and purposes of God. He was wrong, of course, and he is wrong about his plans for you too. He is convinced that he can somehow kill the

HAMAN SEEMED TO HAVE CONTROL OVER THE KINGDOM, BUT HIS TREACHERY WAS ALSO REVEALED, AND HE WAS HANGED ON THE VERY GALLOWS HE HAD PREPARED FOR MORDECAI!

seed God has placed in you, and, thus, stop you from doing anything for God. I declare to you that Satan is a liar. You and I are destined for greater things in the earth.

We know how the story ended in Esther's day, and this should bring us great joy. Bigthan and Teresh seemed to have a foolproof plan in place, but God revealed it to Mordecai, and the plot was foiled. Haman seemed to have control over the kingdom, but his treachery was also revealed, and he was hanged on the very gallows he had prepared for Mordecai. To this day, the Jewish people celebrate these events.

You should celebrate too. You are God's chosen one, and He has declared that nothing will hinder you. No weapon formed against you—none—will prosper. Period!

In time, the record book was opened and the mighty deeds of Mordecai were rewarded. Get ready, beloved, for your time has come too. A seed always results in a harvest.

PART IV

Understanding the Principle of
Sowing in a Time of Famine

CHAPTER 15

Sowing by Faith in Difficult Times

> *Then Isaac sowed seed in that land and received in the same year a hundred times as much as he had planted, and the LORD favored him with blessings. And the man became great and gained more and more until he became very wealthy and distinguished; he owned flocks, herds, and a great supply of servants, and the Philistines envied him.* Genesis 26:12-14

Now that we understand seed and what it produces, what Isaac did in Genesis 26 makes more sense to us. He sowed seed and reaped a harvest. In other words, he put something into motion that was destined to bring forth growth and development, and he immediately became fruitful. The interesting thing here is that Isaac sowed his seed in a time of famine. It was not a good time to sow seeds, but he sowed them anyway because he believed in the God of harvest.

Many of you know what it's like to be in a famine. During a prolonged drought the ground becomes dry and hard and does not produce as it normally would. This means that cattle and other livestock often die or have to be slaughtered prematurely because there is not enough food for them. People also die in such times because not enough food is being produced to support everyone, or food cannot be properly transported to the places it is needed.

Droughts bring difficult times for all concerned. It is certainly not a time to think about sowing seed in the normal way, and yet that's exactly what Isaac did. Isaac sowed his seed in faith, believing that because God had told him not to go to Egypt, He would provide for him where he was. And when he sowed his seed, he put something into motion that was destined to bring forth growth and development. And he was not disappointed.

Friend, the minute you sow your seed — giving, lending a hand, showing kindness, etc. — something always happens. As we have noted, it may not be immediately visible to your

DROUGHTS BRING DIFFICULT TIMES FOR ALL CONCERNED. IT IS CERTAINLY NOT A TIME TO THINK ABOUT SOWING SEED IN THE NORMAL WAY, AND YET THAT'S EXACTLY WHAT ISAAC DID!

natural eye, but the minute you sow, something is set in motion.

Isaac sowed his seed by faith, and despite the difficult circumstances of the time, he also reaped. Sowing always brings reaping. Isaac's reaping was miraculous. Scientists cite 3 to 1 as the minimum crop yield needed to sustain life. Isaac reaped 100 to 1:

> *Then Isaac sowed seed in that land and received in the same year a hundred times as much as he had planted.* Genesis 26:12

When Isaac sowed, he reaped. He reaped a hundredfold. Get ready to reap your hundredfold harvest as well.

At this moment, you are standing at the door of your destiny, and a new threshold and a hundredfold blessing will be your portion as you begin to understand the seed and the sowing of yourself and the sowing of your seed into the right soil. This means not on stoney ground and not among thorns or thistles. But let your life be one that is pliable and properly tilled, a fertile ground from which God can bring forth a rich harvest.

Isaac reaped 100 to 1, a hundredfold reward, but what else was granted to him for his faithful sowing?

Sowing by Faith in Difficult Times

The LORD favored him with blessings.

Genesis 26:12

Wow! God's favor is intended to be your portion. The seeds are falling. Are you receiving them?

When God's favor comes upon you, it changes everything. Before, maybe no one wanted to hear from you. But when God's favor comes, your voice will not only go forth to the nations; it will be heard. You will teach under the anointing of the Most High because of His favor. Knowing that favor will be your portion, you should be excited about sowing your seed.

And what is it that you will be favored with? With God's blessings.

What came next for Isaac?

And the man became great.   Genesis 26:13

Let me declare to you that there is greatness hidden in you. Seeds of greatness have been deposited in you. Greatness comes with sowing. Have you sowed your seed? Have you done it in faith? Are you expecting a miraculous harvest?

What else happened to Isaac as a result of being blessed and favored by God?

WHETHER IT IS IN
BLESSING YOU WITH
GREAT NATURAL
WEALTH OR GRANTING
YOU AN OVERFLOW OF
THE RICHES OF HEAVEN,
LIKE ISAAC, GOD
WANTS YOU TO BECOME
"DISTINGUISHED!"

[He] gained more and more until he became very wealthy and distinguished.   Genesis 26:13

"He became very wealthy and distinguished." The word *wealth* can be deceptive. We can be the richest people on the face of the earth without having a lot of earthly riches. Whether it is in blessing you with great natural wealth or granting you an overflow of the riches of Heaven, like Isaac, God wants you to become *"distinguished."* You will stand tall among others. Believe God for it.

God has chosen to co-labor with men and women. He doesn't use angels in this same way. You must be His voice in the earth. And when He raises you up, you suddenly become great in His Kingdom. The Scriptures declare:

Eye hath not seen, nor ear heard, neither have entered into the heart of man, the things which God hath prepared for them that love him.
                    1 Corinthians 2:9, KJV

And we know that all things work together for good to them that love God, to them who are the called according to his purpose.
                        Romans 8:28, KJV

If you are one of those who love God, we might say 1 Corinthians 24:9 this way: "Eye hath not seen, nor ear heard, neither has entered into the heart of man, the greatness which God hath prepared for YOU." We might say Romans 8:28 this way: "And we know that all things work together for good to YOU who love God, to YOU who are the called according to His purpose." Yes, greatness is your portion, and you will be known throughout the earth.

One night, as I lay on my bed meditating on these things, specific faces came before me. I knew some of them, and some of them I didn't. You may have been one of them. God has great things prepared for you, just as He did for Isaac of old. Get ready, for it will be more than you could ever imagine.

What came upon Isaac when he sowed? Favor and greatness, and he was distinguished among the men of the earth and full of the blessing of God. Again, that thirteenth verse declares:

And the man became great and gained more and more until he became very wealthy and distinguished.

We don't come to God to get wealth, but when He sows into us and then we become sowers as

134

WE MIGHT SAY ROMANS 8:28 THIS WAY: "AND WE KNOW THAT ALL THINGS WORK TOGETHER FOR GOOD TO YOU WHO LOVE GOD, TO YOU WHO ARE THE CALLED ACCORDING TO HIS PURPOSE!"

well, wealth becomes our portion. Get ready to receive all that is yours.

Isaac became very distinguished, and you can be too. Get ready to reap the rewards of sowing, and your harvest will be great, as was Isaac's.

PART V

In Conclusion

CHAPTER 16

The Importance of Having an Ear to Hear

*And He said, He who has ears to hear, let him
be hearing [and let him consider, and compre-
hend].*   Mark 4:9

Jesus ended the Parable of the Sower and the
Seed with these amazing words. But doesn't
everyone who has ears hear? Definitely not.
And, what's more, few bother to *"consider and
comprehend."*

It's a shame that we have to give such elemen-
tary teachings, but it's necessary because many
just don't get it. At the very least, they don't have
the revelation of it. Hearing and understanding
are two completely different things. Many don't

bother to listen. Others listen but fail to understand. Relatively few bother to *"consider and comprehend."*

Why is this so important? Because this is the way God's Kingdom operates. Seeds are sown into you, and it's up to you what you do with them. As we have seen, right now, through the pages of this book, seed is being sown into your heart. Don't let it fall to the ground and die. Plant it deep in good soil and believe for it to produce the amazing harvest it's capable of producing.

The seeds being sown into your life go far beyond the words that are printed on these pages. The Spirit of the Most High God is sowing into your life even now, and His anticipation is a great harvest. If you can get a revelation of these seeds and their potential, your life will be transformed.

Why is the Sower sowing seeds into your life? He desires to put into motion something that you, too, have been longing to see. You have long known it was yours, but you didn't quite know how to lay hold of it. Now, put those seeds into deep soil and watch what God will do with them. Have an ear to hear what the Spirit is saying!

THE SEEDS BEING SOWN
INTO YOUR LIFE GO FAR
BEYOND THE WORDS
THAT ARE PRINTED ON
THESE PAGES!

CHAPTER 17

Will You Become a Sower?

They who sow in tears shall reap in joy and singing.
He who goes forth bearing seed and weeping [at needing his precious supply of grain for sowing] shall doubtless come again with rejoicing, bringing his sheaves with him.　　　Psalm 126:5-6

Well, it's up to you now. Do you understand better the power of the seed? Will you sow more than you have in the past? Will you sow in faith, knowing that it is God who blesses the seed and makes it fruitful? I trust that you will. This is your promise:

They who sow in tears shall reap in joy and singing.

He who goes forth bearing seed and weeping [at needing his precious supply of grain for sowing] shall doubtless come again with rejoicing, bringing his sheaves with him.

Amen!

Author Contact

You may contact Andy McDougal directly for conferences, retreats, missionary projects and church and house meetings. She is a gifted prophetess who will lift you and your people into the realms of glory.

AndysMinistry@gmail.com

www.facebook.com/andrea.mcdougal.3
www.facebook.com/andymcdougalministries

Phone: 225-572-9844

Other Books by Andy McDougal

THE
GLORY
OF
GOD
REVEALED

The What, the Why and the How of the
Current Revival of Signs and Wonders

Andrea "Andy" McDougal

HIS WONDERS IN THE DEEP

IN THE

DEEP

GOD'S CALL
TO THE SUPERNATURAL

Andrea "Andy" McDougal

YOUR Camels Are Coming

The Bride's Journey
to
Destiny

Andrea "Andy" McDougal

The
ARROWS
of the
LORD

Andrea "Andy" McDougal

A Southern Lady's Tea Journey

A Legacy

Andrea "Andy" McDougal

A Southern Lady's Tea Adventures

Andrea "Andy" McDougal

www.ingramcontent.com/pod-product-compliance
Lightning Source LLC
Chambersburg PA
CBHW021110130626
46554CB00002B/622